sharks

Written by Janine Amos
Reading consultants: Christopher Collier and Alan Howe,
Bath Spa University, UK

First published by Parragon in 2008
Parragon
Queen Street House
4 Queen Street
Bath BA1 1HE, UK

ISBN 978-1-4075-1836-7

Printed in China

sharks

Bath · New York · Singapore · Hong Kong · Cologne · Delhi · Melbourne

Parents' notes

This book is part of a series of non-fiction books designed to appeal to children learning to read.

Each book has been developed with the help of educational experts.

At the end of each book is a quiz to help your child remember the information and the meanings of some of the words and sentences. There is also a glossary of difficult words relating to the subject matter in the book, and an index.

Contents

What is a shark?

Sharks are fish that live in seas and oceans across the world. Some sharks are tiny, others are giants. Some are gentle and some are fierce.

Sharks don't have bones. Their skeletons are made from light, stretchy cartilage.

fins

jaws

gills

Sharks breathe through slits called gills.

There are hundreds of kinds of sharks. Here are just three of them.

Wobbegongs hide on the ocean floor. They are well camouflaged.

Dogfish have long, slim bodies to slip through the water.

tail

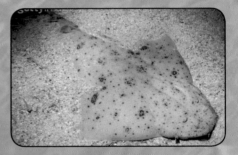

Angel sharks have flat bodies. They also hide on the ocean floor.

DiscoveryFact™

Sharks have been living on Earth for 400 million years. They were around at the time of the dinosaurs.

Amazing sharks

Can you imagine a fish that has a head shaped like a hammer? Or one that can gobble up a sea lion whole? Sharks are some of the world's most amazing creatures.

The bullet-shaped mako shark is the fastest fish in the ocean. It can swim at 45 miles per hour.

The strange hammerhead shark has eyes on each side of its head. It swings its head from side to side to get an all-around view.

The great white shark eats other sharks for dinner—along with whole penguins, seals, and sea lions.

The gentle whale shark is the world's biggest fish. It weighs as much as two elephants.

Teeth and tails

Teeth and tails are two of a shark's most important weapons. They are designed to help it catch prey.

Sharks always have a mouth full of teeth. When one set of teeth wears out, there is another set waiting.

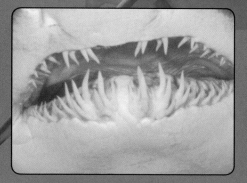

A nurse shark has long, curved teeth for hooking prey.

A shark's tail helps push it along. Fast swimmers have curved tails. The thresher shark has a long, strong tail to knock out its prey.

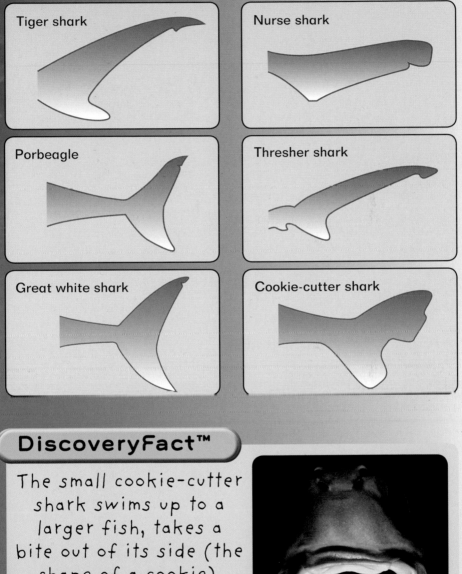

Tiger shark

Nurse shark

Porbeagle

Thresher shark

Great white shark

Cookie-cutter shark

DiscoveryFact™

The small cookie-cutter shark swims up to a larger fish, takes a bite out of its side (the shape of a cookie), and swims away again very quickly!

Swimming

Most sharks are graceful and powerful swimmers. Their smooth bodies are perfect for moving underwater. Sharks swim in S-shaped movements, powered by their tails.

Fins on each side of a shark's body help it steer.

The stiff fin on a shark's back helps with balance.

The shark's long tail beats from side to side, pushing the shark forward through the water.

Inside most fish is an air-filled swimbladder. It keeps the fish afloat. Sharks don't have swimbladders. Most have to keep swimming or they sink.

The prehistoric shark *Megalodon* may have been up to 65 feet long. Here is one of its huge teeth next to the tooth of a modern shark.

Blue shark

The blue shark is a long-distance traveler. It swims hundreds of miles every year, searching for food or to mate.

The blue shark has a bright-blue back and a white tummy. These colors help to hide it in the ocean.

Blue sharks hunt with their mouths wide open, trapping fish in the corners. They are slow swimmers but can move very quickly when they attack.

One blue shark made a trip of almost 4,500 miles from New York to Brazil. That's a lot of swimming!

The blue shark feeds on small fish, such as sardines, and on squid (shown left). It lives in warm and cool oceans all over the world.

Hunting

Sharks are always seeking out their next meal. They can see, hear, touch, and smell, just like people. But their senses are much more powerful.

Touch
A lateral line along their sides helps sharks pick up movements in the water around them.

Hearing
A shark's ears can hear sounds traveling through the water.

gills   wobbegong   dogfish   angel shark   fin

great white   hammerhead   whale shark   mako

nurse shark   cookie-cutter shark   *Megalodon* tooth

blue shark   squid   tail   dinosaur   pup   teeth

killer whale   seal pup   mermaid's purse   stingray

submarine   penguins   surfboard   sea lion   friends

An extra sense lets sharks pick up the electric signals given off by fish. This sense is particularly powerful in hammerhead sharks.

Sight
A shark's eyes can see well in dim underwater light.

Smell
Sharks have good noses. They can sniff out blood half a mile away.

Great white

Great white sharks are giant hunters. They feed on animals such as sea lions and seals, as well as on smaller sharks.

Newborn great whites are already 5 feet long. Young sharks eat other fish, such as mackerel and tuna.

Great whites swim near the surface to hunt. But they can dive deeper than a submarine.

Great whites have 3,000 teeth. Each one is about as long as your finger.

DiscoveryFact™

A killer whale like this, and people, are a great white's only enemies.

Family life

All baby sharks are born from eggs. The eggs of most sharks grow inside their mother. A few kinds of shark lay their eggs on the ocean floor, safe inside tough egg cases.

Shark babies are called pups.

A blue shark mother can give birth to 50 or more babies at a time.

Dogfish eggs are protected by an egg case called a mermaid's purse. The babies grow inside, feeding on the egg yolk.

Lemon shark eggs grow inside their mother. She gives birth to tiny pups, which soon swim off to find food.

Hammerhead

The hammerhead's flat, T-shaped head makes it look different from any other shark. Hammerheads swim together in groups called schools.

Most hammerheads live in warm oceans, off the coast of Australia and Central America.

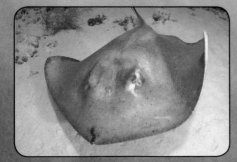

The hammerhead's favorite food is the stingray. It holds the ray down with its "hammer" and takes a bite.

Baby hammerheads are born with their heads bent backward, so they don't get stuck inside their mother.

Hammerheads swing their heads from side to side as they swim, picking up smells and sounds in the water.

Their eyes are far apart on their huge heads.

Are sharks dangerous?

Most sharks don't eat people. But some sharks, such as the great white, the bull shark, and the tiger shark do attack. There are fewer than 100 attacks every year worldwide.

To stay safe, swim with your friends. Never swim if you are bleeding, because blood attracts sharks.

People are putting sharks in danger. We kill them for food and for sport.

If you see a fin above the water looking like this it means that a shark is near you.

A swimmer on a surfboard can look like a seal— to a shark.

Quiz

Now try this quiz!
All the answers can be found in this book.

How long have sharks been living on Earth?

(a) 40 years
(b) 400 years
(c) 400 million years

Which shark is the fastest fish in the ocean?

(a) The mako shark
(b) The great white
(c) The wobbegong

Which parts of a shark's body help it steer?

(a) The fins
(b) The teeth
(c) The gills

What do young great white sharks eat?

(a) Plants
(b) Fish
(c) Penguins

What is a hammerhead shark's favorite food?

(a) Chocolate
(b) Seaweed
(c) Stingrays

What are baby sharks called?

(a) Pups
(b) Fry
(c) Spawn

Glossary

Cartilage	Strong, stretchy material that forms a shark's skeleton.
Fins	The wing-like parts of a fish that help it steer and balance.
Gills	The parts inside a shark's throat that let it breathe in water.
Lateral line	A line of tiny hairs along a shark's body. The lateral line picks up movements in the water.
Mate	To pair up in order to make babies.
Mermaid's purse	The egg case of a dogfish. At first the cases are soft. They soon become hard and will protect the egg.

Prey	The animals that a shark hunts and eats.
Pups	Newborn sharks.
Senses	To see, hear, taste, touch, and smell. Sharks have an extra sense for picking up electrical signals from their prey.
Stingray	A type of fish with poisonous spines on its tail. Rays are the cousins of sharks.
Swimbladder	A tiny air-filled bag that helps some fish to float. Sharks don't have swimbladders.
Yolk	The yellow part of an egg that feeds the growing baby shark.

Index

m

mako sharks 8
mate 14
Megalodon 13
mermaid's purses 21
mothers 20, 21, 23

n

nurse sharks 10, 11

o

ocean floor 7, 20

p

porbeagles 11
prey 10, 11
pups (babies) 18, 20-21, 23

s

schools 22
senses 16-17
sight 16
skeletons 6
smell 17, 23
steering 12
stingrays 22
surfboards 25
swimbladders 13
swimming 8, 11, 12-13, 14, 15, 19, 23, 24

t

tails 7, 10, 11, 12, 13
teeth 10, 13, 19
thresher sharks 11
tiger sharks 11, 24
touch 16

w

whale sharks 9
wobbegongs 7

y

yolk 21

Acknowledgments

t=top, c=center, b=bottom, r=right, l=left

Cover: Denis Scott/Corbis

p.3 Denis Scott/Corbis, p.4 Tim Davis/Corbis, p.5tl Jeffrey L.Rotman/ Corbis, p.5m Denis Scott/Corbis , p.5b Amos Nachoum/Corbis, p.6-7 Tim Davis/Corbis, p.6 DLILLC/Corbis, p.7tl Jeffrey L.Rotman/Corbis, p.7tr P.Ginet-Drin/Photocuisine/Corbis, p.7m Norbert Wu/Getty Images, p.8bl Denis Scott/Corbis, p.9tr Tim Davis/Corbis, p.9bl Louie Psihoyos/Corbis, p.10 Denis Scott/Corbis, p.10bl Gary Bell/Zefa/ Corbis, p.11br Getty Images/National Geographic Creative, p.12-13 Carson Ganci/Design Pics/Corbis, p.13ml Tim Davis/Corbis, p.13br Jeffrey L.Rotman/Corbis, p.14-15 Background Ralph A. Clevenger/ Corbis, p.14-15 Amos Nachoum/Corbis, p.15bl Jeffrey L.Rotman/Corbis, p.16-17 Jeffrey L.Rotman/Corbis, p.16bl Jeffrey L.Rotman/Corbis, p.16br Stephen Frink/Corbis, p.17tr Denis Scott/Corbis, p.17bl P.Ginet-Drin/Photocuisine/Corbis, p.17br Stuart Westmorland/Corbis, p.18-19 DLILLC/Corbis, p.18br Amos Nachoum/Corbis, p.19tr Stephen Frink/ Corbis, 19br Tom Brakefield/Corbis, 20 Tobias Bernhard/zefa/Corbis, 21ml Douglas P.Wilson; Frank Lane Picture Agency/Corbis, 21br Douglas P.Wilson; Frank Lane Picture Agency/Corbis, 22-23 Denis Scott/Corbis, 22b Carson Ganci/Design Pics/Corbis,l 23tr Jeffrey L.Rotman/Corbis, 24-25 Creasource/Corbis, 25br Rick Doyle/Corbis, 25tl Dimaggio/ Kalish/Corbis, 25tr DLILLC/Corbis, 27t Amos NachoumCorbis,

Additional images used on sticker sheet: Third row, fifth picture: Gavriel Jecan/Corbis, Fourth row, sixth picture: Bernard Brenton/ Dreamstime, Fourth row, seventh picture: Stuart Westmorland/Corbis, Sixth row, second picture: Philip Perry; Frank Lane Picture Agency/ Corbis